HAL LEONARD DRUMSET METHOD SONGBOOK

AUDIO ACCESS INCLUDED

T0087118

PLAYBACK+
Speed • Pitch • Balance • Loop

To access audio visit:
www.halleonard.com/mylibrary

Enter Code
7328-2921-6686-3425

ISBN 978-1-5400-6035-8

For all works contained herein:
Unauthorized copying, arranging, adapting, recording, Internet posting, public performance,
or other distribution of the music in this publication is an infringement of copyright.
Infringers are liable under the law.

Visit Hal Leonard Online at
www.halleonard.com

Contact us:
Hal Leonard
7777 West Bluemound Road
Milwaukee, WI 53213
Email: info@halleonard.com

In Europe, contact:
Hal Leonard Europe Limited
42 Wigmore Street
Marylebone, London, W1U 2RN
Email: info@halleonardeurope.com

In Australia, contact:
Hal Leonard Australia Pty. Ltd.
4 Lentara Court
Cheltenham, Victoria, 3192 Australia
Email: info@halleonard.com.au

CONTENTS

BILLIE JEAN

Words and Music by Michael Jackson

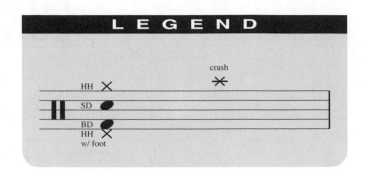

Intro
Moderately ♩ = 117

(Bass enters)

(4) (8)

(Strings enter) (4)

Verse

She was more like a beau - ty queen...

(4) (8)

(12)

Verse

She told me her name was Bil - lie Jean... (4)

Copyright © 1982 Mijac Music
All Rights Administered by Sony/ATV Music Publishing LLC, 424 Church Street, Suite 1200, Nashville, TN 37219
International Copyright Secured   All Rights Reserved

Verse

She told my ba-by we danced till three...

Pre-Chorus

Peo-ple al-ways told _ me...

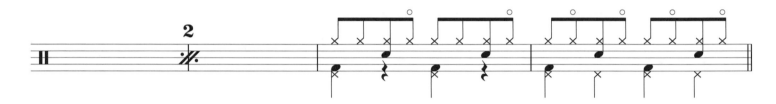

Chorus

Bil-lie Jean   is   not my   lov - er...

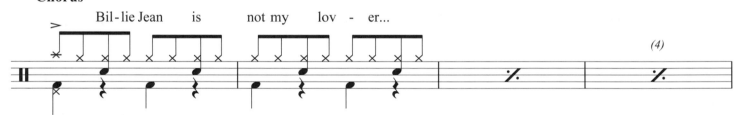

Chorus

Bil-lie Jean   is   not my   lov - er...

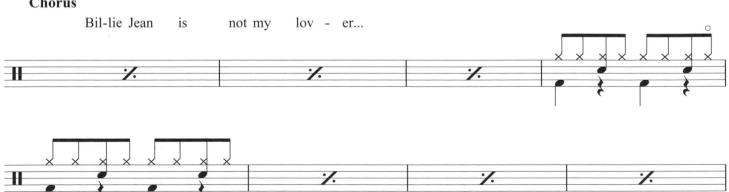

Get Down On It

Words and Music by Ronald Bell, James Taylor, George Brown,
Robert Bell, Claydes Smith, Spike Mickens and Eumir Deodato

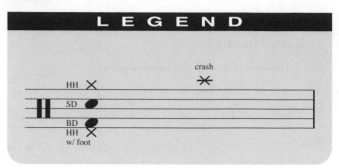

Intro
Moderately ♩ = 112

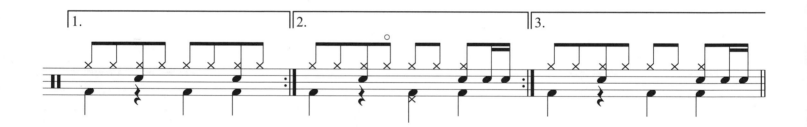

Chorus

Get down on it...

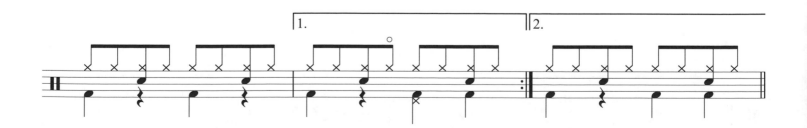

© 1981 WARNER-TAMERLANE PUBLISHING CORP., OLD RIVER MUSIC and WC MUSIC CORP.
All Rights for OLD RIVER MUSIC Administered by WARNER-TAMERLANE PUBLISHING CORP.
All Rights Reserved   Used by Permission

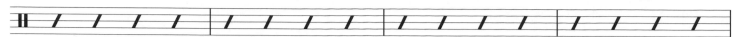

(8)

Intro

(4)

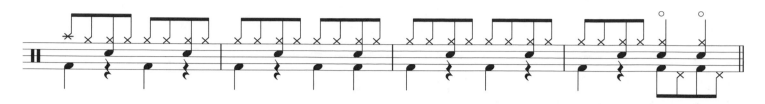

(8)

Chorus

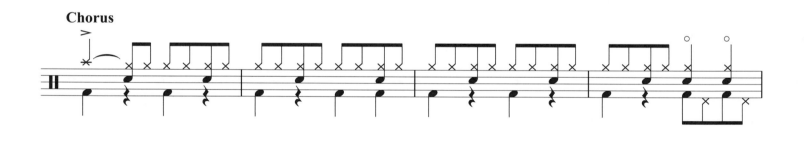

Outro-Chorus

(4)

Repeat and fade

(8)

JUST MY IMAGINATION
(RUNNING AWAY WITH ME)

Words and Music by Norman Whitfield
and Barrett Strong

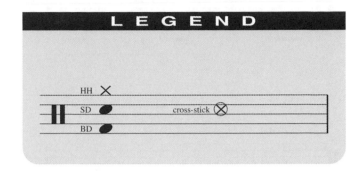

Intro
Moderately ♩ = 90

Verse

Copyright © 1970 Jobete Music Co., Inc.
Copyright Renewed
All Rights Administered by Sony/ATV Music Publishing LLC on behalf of
Stone Agate Music (A Division of Jobete Music Co., Inc.), 424 Church Street, Suite 1200, Nashville, TN 37219
International Copyright Secured   All Rights Reserved

Chorus

...just my im-ag - i - na - tion...

Bridge

Chorus

Repeat and fade

This page has been intentionally left blank to facilitate page turns.

SHE WILL BE LOVED

Words and Music by Adam Levine
and James Valentine

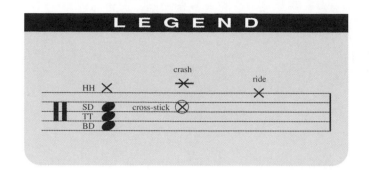

Intro
Moderately ♩ = 102

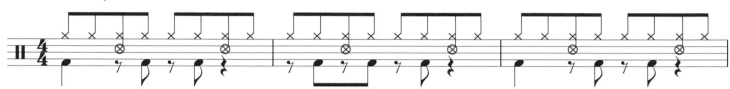

Verse

Beau-ty queen of   on - ly   eight - teen...

Pre-Chorus

I drove for   miles

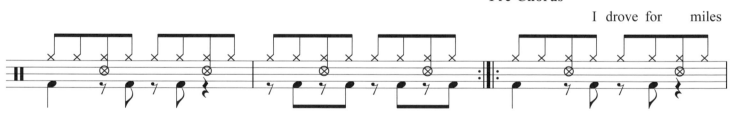

and   miles...

1.

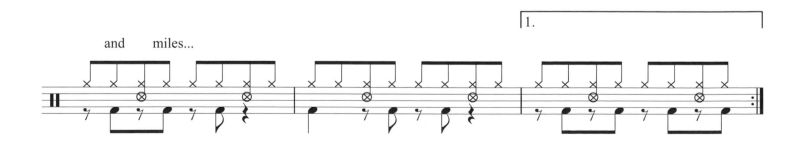

Copyright © 2002 by Universal Music - MGB Songs, Valentine Valentine, Universal Music - Careers
and February Twenty Second Music
All Rights for Valentine Valentine in the United States Administered by Universal Music - MGB Songs
All Rights for February Twenty Second Music in the United States Administered by Universal Music - Careers
International Copyright Secured   All Rights Reserved

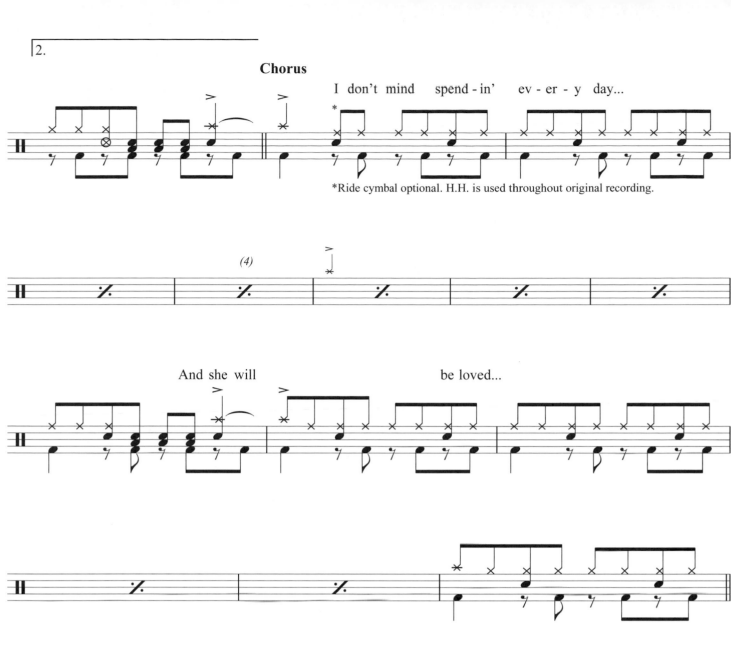

Chorus

I don't mind spend-in' ev-er-y day...

*Ride cymbal optional. H.H. is used throughout original recording.

And she will be loved...

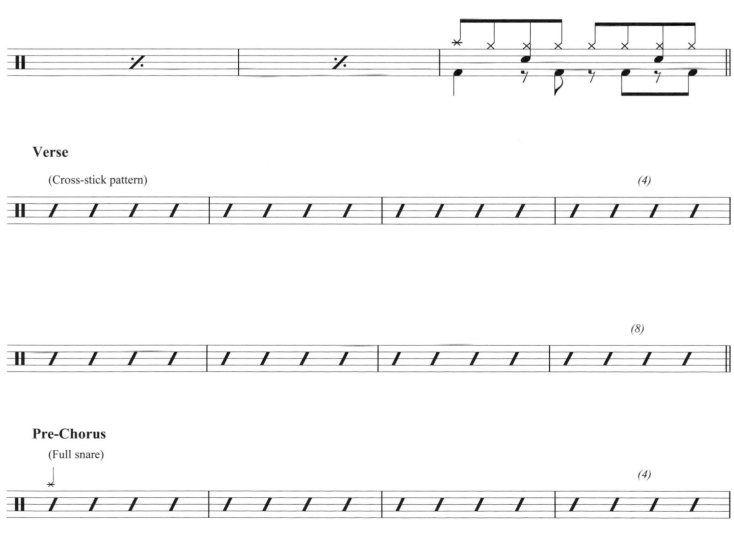

Verse

(Cross-stick pattern)

(4)

(8)

Pre-Chorus

(Full snare)

(4)

Chorus

I don't mind spend-in' ev-er-y day...

(4)

And she will

be loved...

Bridge

I know where you hide...

(4)

(4)

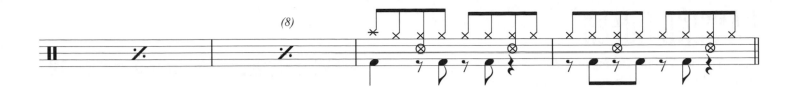

Verse

Tap on my win-dow...

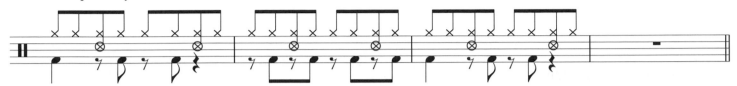

Chorus

I don't mind spend-in' ev-er-y day...

And she will

Outro-Chorus

be loved...

1., 2., 3.   4.

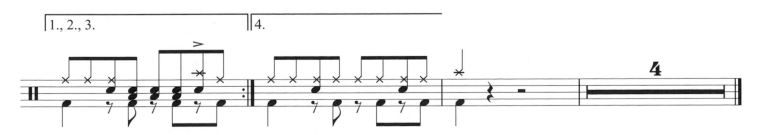

DANCING QUEEN

Words and Music by Benny Andersson,
Bjorn Ulvaeus and Stig Anderson

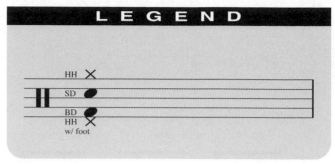

Intro
Moderate Disco ♩ = 100

Chorus
You   can dance...

Copyright © 1976, 1977 UNIVERSAL/UNION SONGS MUSIKFORLAG AB
Copyright Renewed
All Rights Administered by UNIVERSAL - POLYGRAM INTERNATIONAL PUBLISHING, INC. and EMI GROVE PARK MUSIC, INC.
All Rights Reserved   Used by Permission

Verse

Fri - day night...

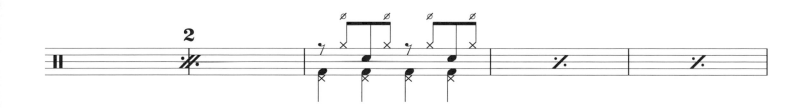

Chorus

You are the danc - ing queen...

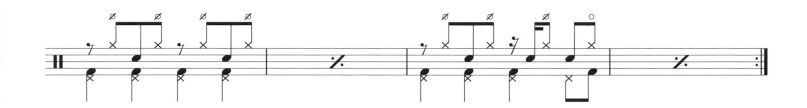

2

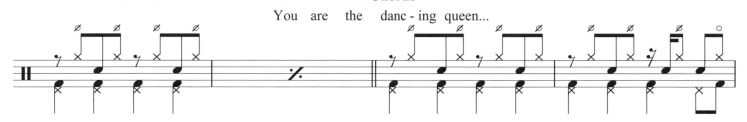

You can dance...

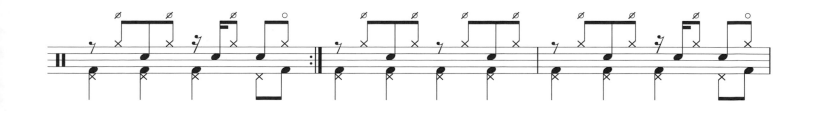

Verse

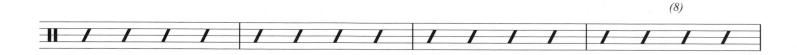

Chorus

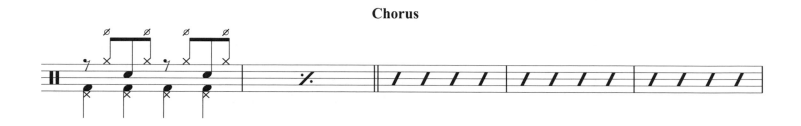

Outro

Repeat and fade

SEPTEMBER

Words and Music by Maurice White,
Al McKay and Allee Willis

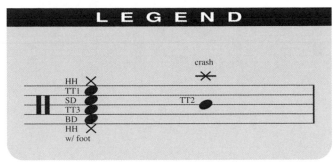

Copyright © 1978 EMI April Music Inc., Steelchest Music, EMI Blackwood Music Inc. and Irving Music Inc.
All Rights Administered by Sony/ATV Music Publishing LLC, 424 Church Street, Suite 1200, Nashville, TN 37219
International Copyright Secured   All Rights Reserved

Chorus

Ba,   dee, yah...

Interlude

Verse

Verse

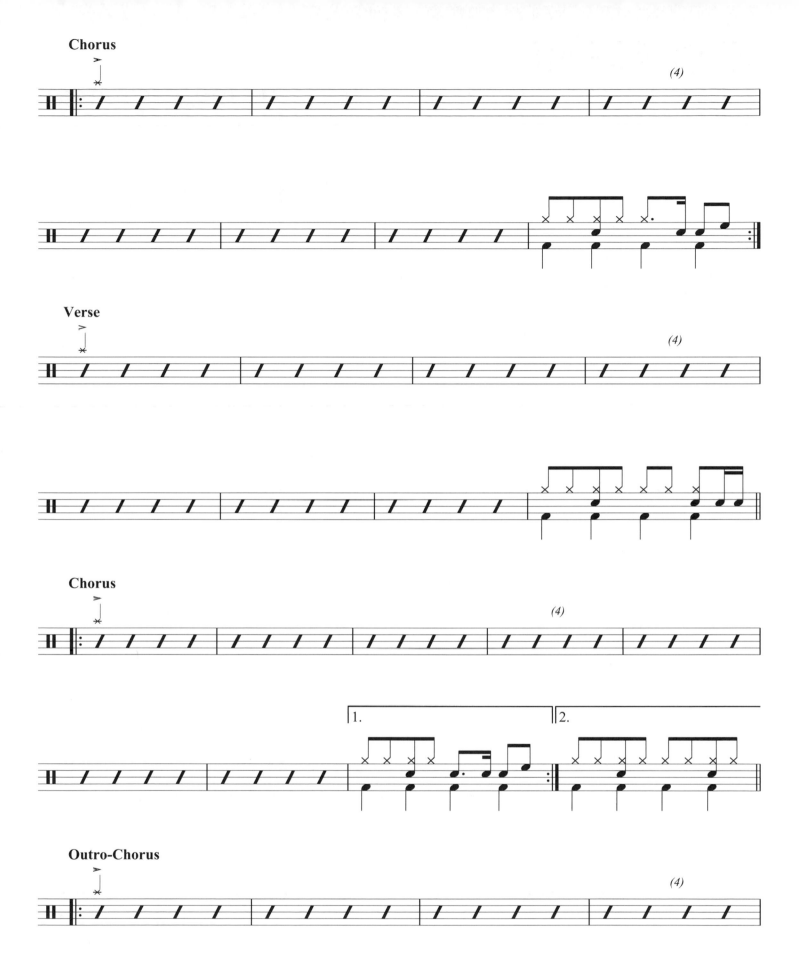

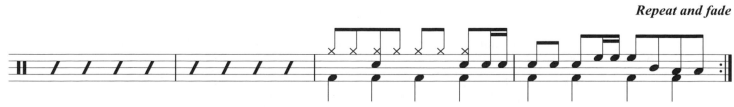

ROLLING IN THE DEEP

Words and Music by Adele Adkins and Paul Epworth

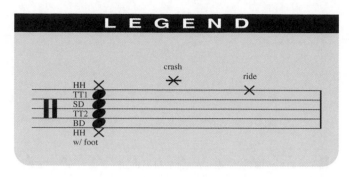

Copyright © 2010, 2011 MELTED STONE PUBLISHING LTD. and EMI MUSIC PUBLISHING LTD.
All Rights for MELTED STONE PUBLISHING LTD. in the U.S. and Canada Controlled and Administered by
UNIVERSAL - SONGS OF POLYGRAM INTERNATIONAL, INC.
All Rights for EMI MUSIC PUBLISHING LTD. Administered by SONY/ATV MUSIC PUBLISHING LLC,
424 Church Street, Suite 1200, Nashville, TN 37219
All Rights Reserved   Used by Permission

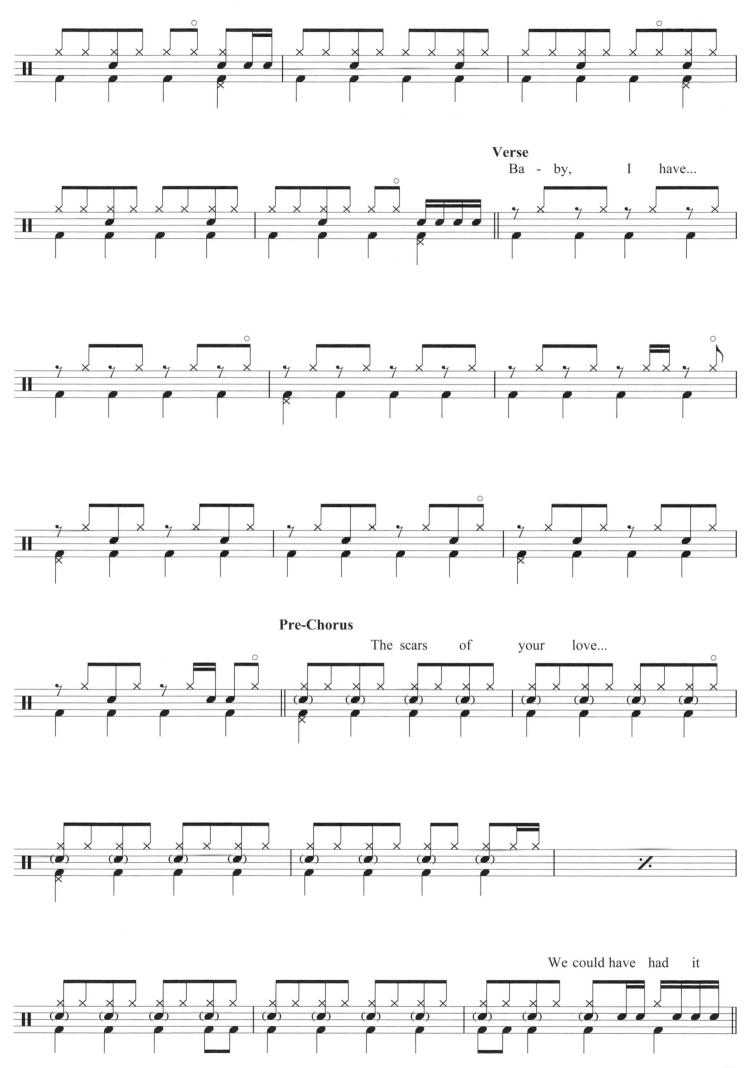

Verse
Ba - by, I have...

Pre-Chorus
The scars of your love...

We could have had it

Bridge

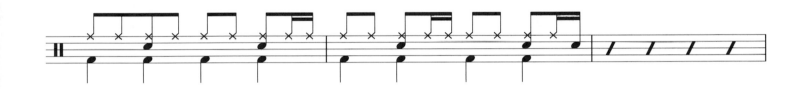

We could have had it all... **Chorus**

(4)

LOCKED OUT OF HEAVEN

Words and Music by Bruno Mars,
Ari Levine and Philip Lawrence

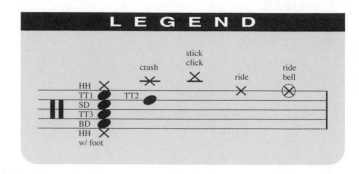

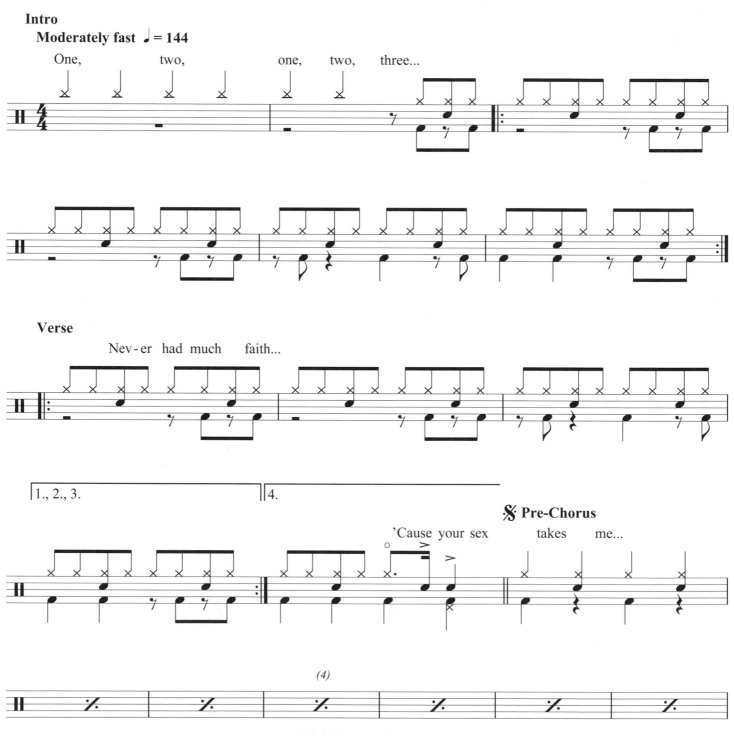

Copyright © 2012 BMG Gold Songs, Mars Force Music, Toy Plane Music, Northside Independent Music Publishing LLC,
Thou Art The Hunger, WC Music Corp., Roc Nation Music and Music Famamenem
All Rights for BMG Gold Songs and Mars Force Music Administered by BMG Rights Management (US) LLC
All Rights for Toy Plane Music Administered by Downtown Music Publishing LLC
All Rights for Thou Art The Hunger Administered by Northside Independent Music Publishing LLC
All Rights for Roc Nation Music and Music Famamenem Administered by WC Music Corp.
All Rights Reserved   Used by Permission

This page has been intentionally left blank to facilitate page turns.

EYE OF THE TIGER
Theme from ROCKY III

Words and Music by Frank Sullivan and Jim Peterik

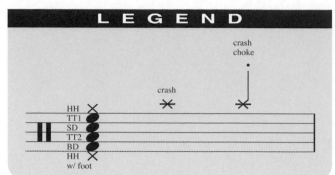

Intro
Moderately ♩ = 108

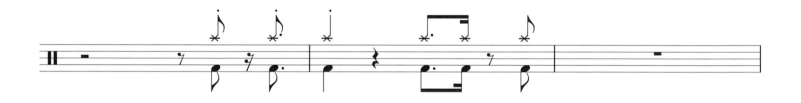

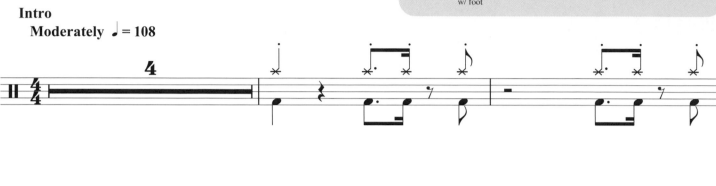

Copyright © 1982 Sony/ATV Music Publishing LLC, Rude Music, Three Wise Boys LLC, WC Music Corp. and Easy Action Music
All Rights on behalf of Sony/ATV Music Publishing LLC, Rude Music and Three Wise Boys LLC Administered by
Sony/ATV Music Publishing LLC, 424 Church Street, Suite 1200, Nashville, TN 37219
All Rights on behalf of Easy Action Music Administered by WC Music Corp.
International Copyright Secured   All Rights Reserved

Verse

Ris - in' up...

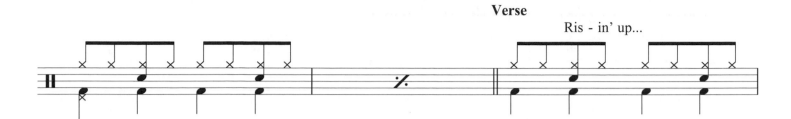

(4)

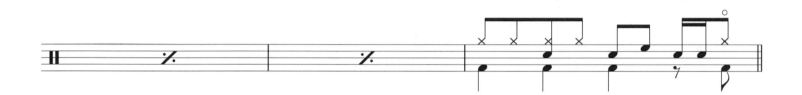

Verse

So man - y times...

(4)

It's   the

Chorus

eye of the ti - ger...

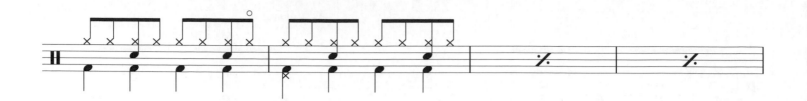

Verse

Face to face...

It's   the

Chorus

eye of the ti - ger...

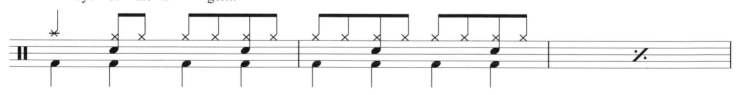

Outro

Repeat and fade

ARMY OF ONE

Words and Music by Christopher Martin,
William Champion, Jonathan Buckland,
Guy Berryman, Tor Hermansen and Mikkel Eriksen

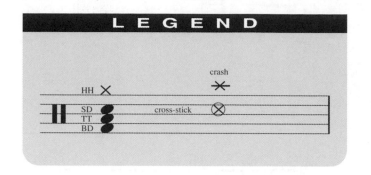

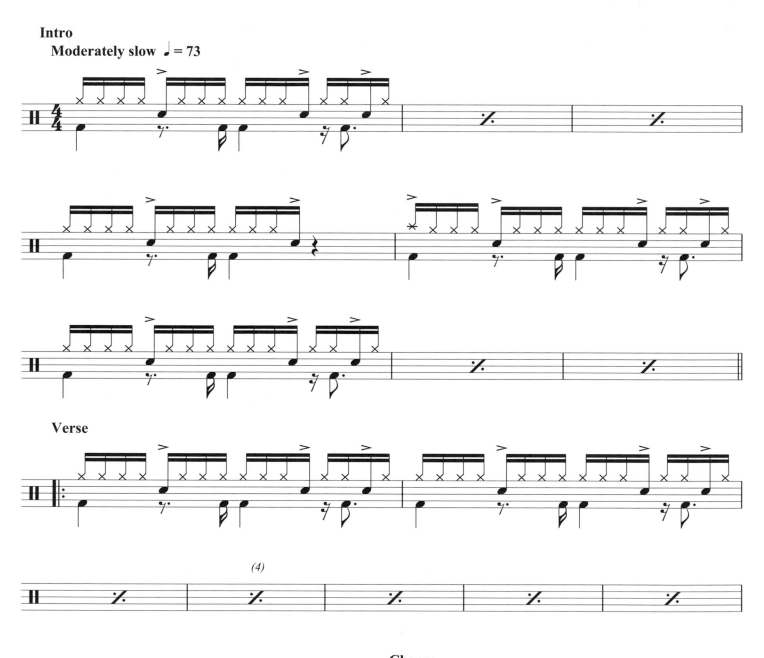

Copyright © 2015 by Universal Music Publishing MGB Ltd. and EMI Music Publishing Ltd.
All Rights for Universal Music Publishing MGB Ltd. in the United States and Canada Administered by Universal Music - MGB Songs
All Rights for EMI Music Publishing Ltd. Administered by Sony/ATV Music Publishing LLC, 424 Church Street,
Suite 1200, Nashville, TN 37219
International Copyright Secured   All Rights Reserved

(4)

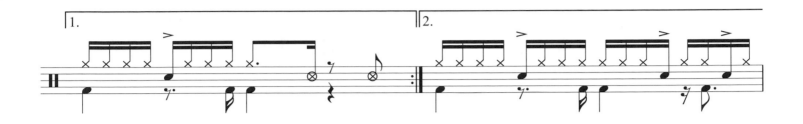

Interlude

Chorus

(4)

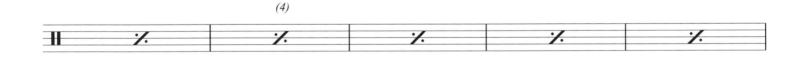

Outro

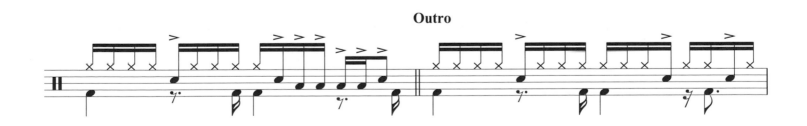

(4)

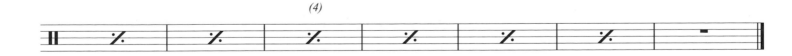

BLACK VELVET

Words and Music by David Tyson
and Christopher Ward

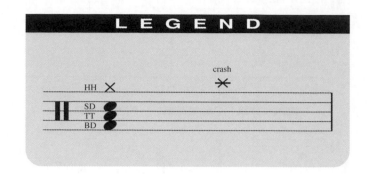

Intro
Moderately ♩ = 91

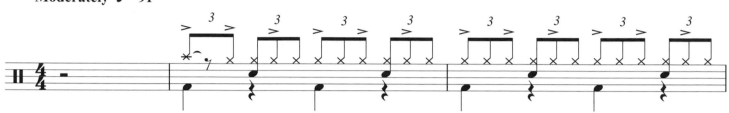

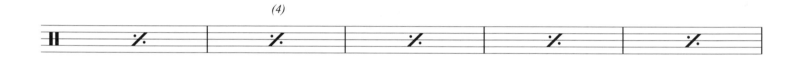

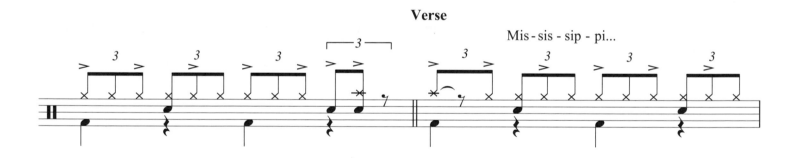

Copyright © 1989 ole Purple Cape Music and Bluebear Waltzes
All Rights for ole Purple Cape Music Administered by Anthem Entertainment
All Rights for Bluebear Waltzes Administered by Kobalt Songs Music Publishing
All Rights Reserved   Used by Permission

Chorus

Black vel - vet...

Black vel - vet if you

please...

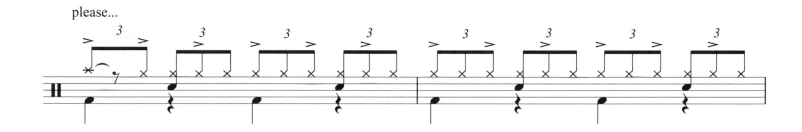

Verse

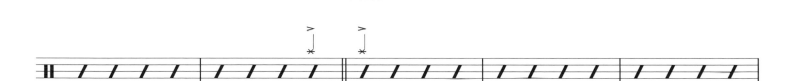

(4)   (8)

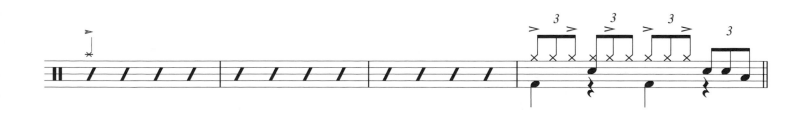

Chorus

Black vel - vet...

Bridge

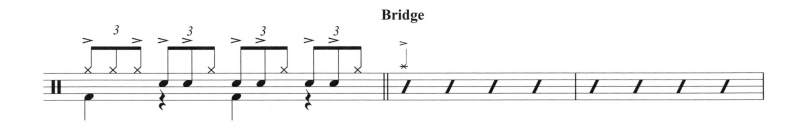

Guitar Solo

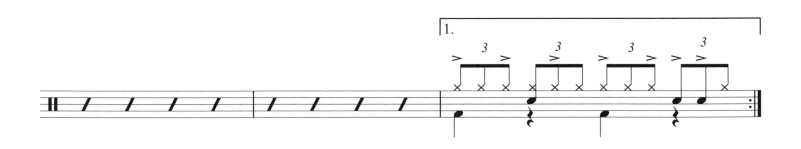

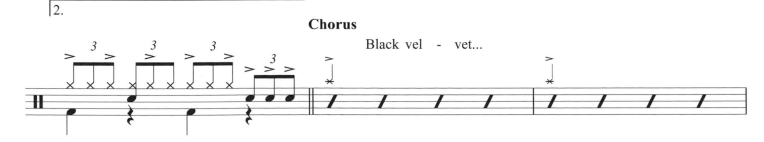

Chorus

Black vel - vet...

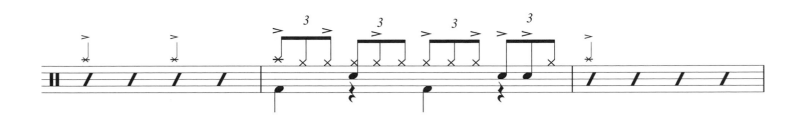

Black vel - vet...

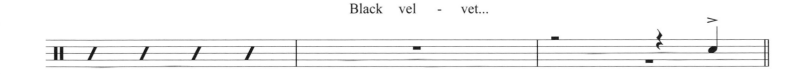

Outro

Repeat and fade

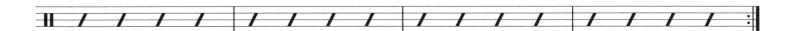

ALL BLUES

By Miles Davis

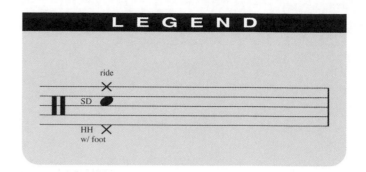

Intro
Slowly ♩. = 45

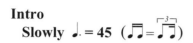

*w/ wire brushes; play snare pattern with right hand and
steady eighth-note swishes on snare with left hand.

Head

Play 16 bars of time   *Play 16 bars of time*

Trumpet Solo

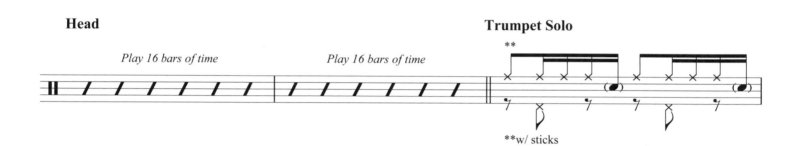

**w/ sticks

Play 11 bars of time   *Play 12 bars of time*   *Play 12 bars of time*

Head

Play 12 bars of time   *Play 4 bars of time*   *Play 16 bars of time*   *Play 16 bars of time*

Outro

Fade out
(4)

Copyright © 1959 Jazz Horn Music Corporation and Miles Davis Properties LLC
Copyright Renewed
All Rights Administered Worldwide by Songs Of Kobalt Music Publishing
All Rights Reserved   Used by Permission

LIVIN' ON A PRAYER

Words and Music by Jon Bon Jovi,
Desmond Child and Richie Sambora

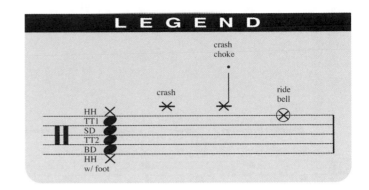

Intro
Moderate Rock ♩ = 122

*Set hi-hat clutch loosely closed.

Verse

Tom - my used to work on the docks...

Copyright © 1986 UNIVERSAL MUSIC PUBLISHING INTERNATIONAL LTD., BON JOVI PUBLISHING,
UNIVERSAL - POLYGRAM INTERNATIONAL PUBLISHING, INC., SONY/ATV MUSIC PUBLISHING LLC and AGGRESSIVE MUSIC
All Rights for UNIVERSAL MUSIC PUBLISHING INTERNATIONAL LTD. and BON JOVI PUBLISHING
Administered by UNIVERSAL MUSIC WORKS
All Rights for SONY/ATV MUSIC PUBLISHING LLC and AGGRESSIVE MUSIC Administered by
SONY/ATV MUSIC PUBLISHING LLC, 424 Church Street, Suite 1200, Nashville, TN 37219
All Rights Reserved   Used by Permission

Pre-Chorus

She says we've got to   hold   on...

Gradually open

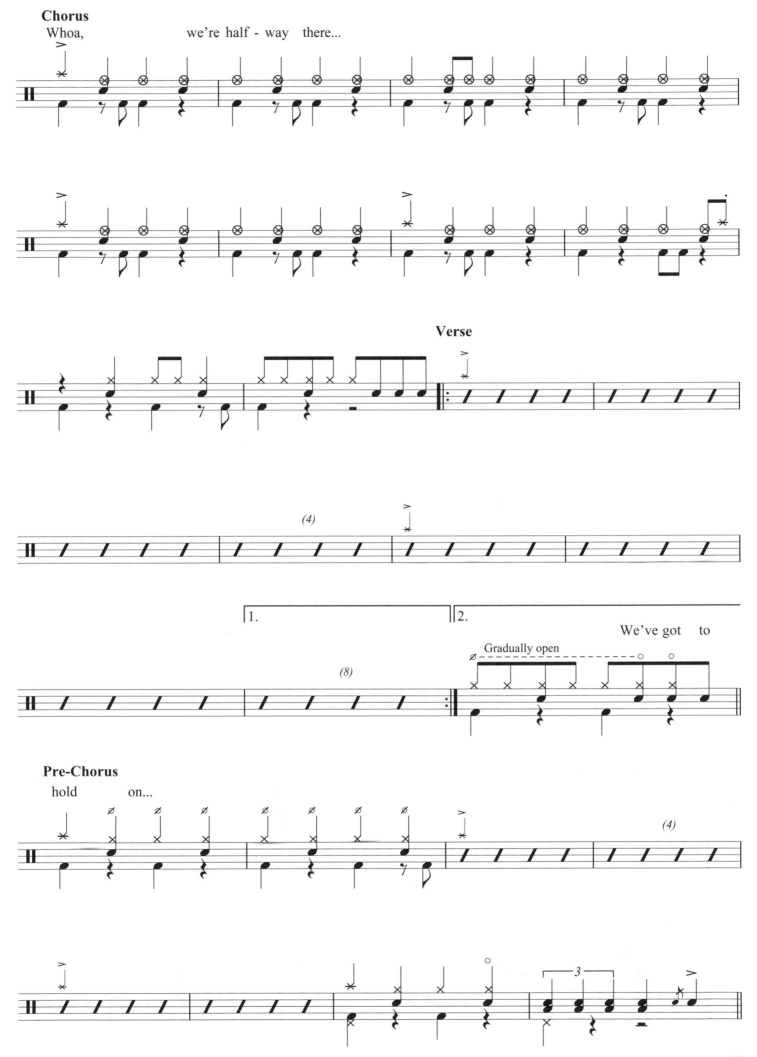

Chorus

Whoa,   we're half - way   there...

Verse

1.   2.

We've got   to

Gradually open

Pre-Chorus

hold   on...

Chorus

Whoa,   we're half - way   there...

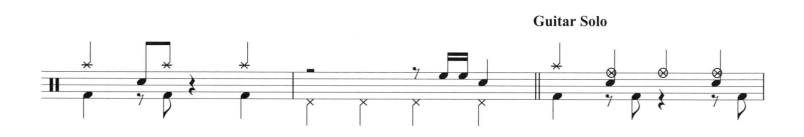

Guitar Solo

Outro-Chorus

Whoa, we're

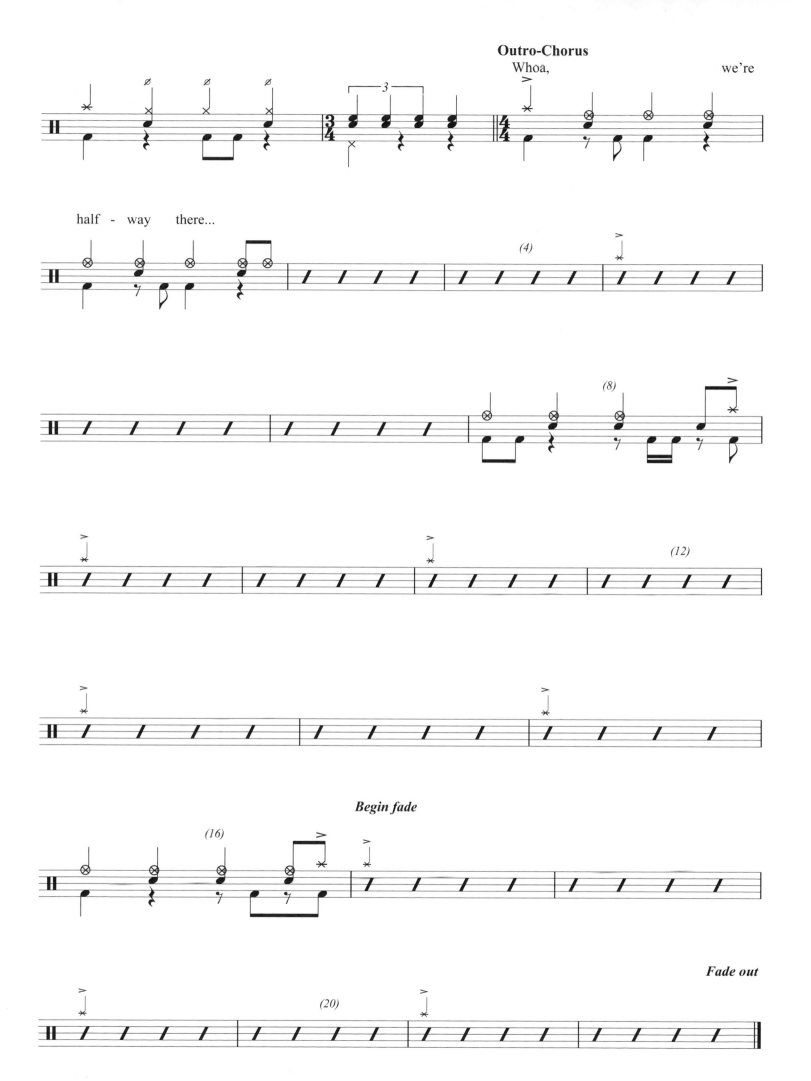

half - way there...

WHAT HURTS THE MOST

Words and Music by Steve Robson and Jeffrey Steele

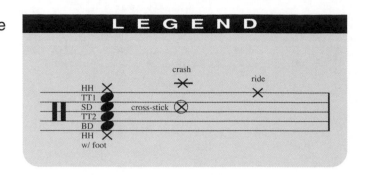

Intro
Slowly ♩ = 68

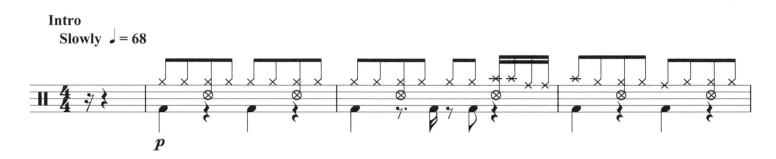

Verse

I can take the rain...

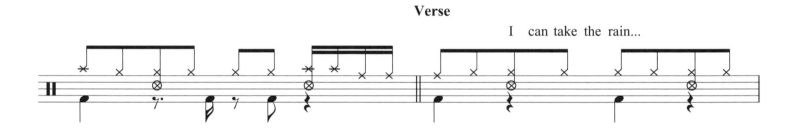

I'm not a-

Pre-Chorus

fraid to cry...

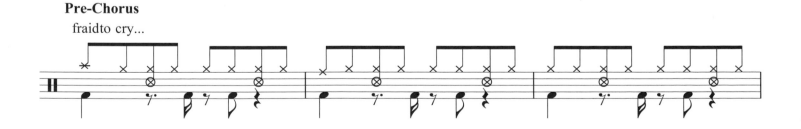

Copyright © 2005 RONDOR MUSIC (LONDON) LTD., SONGS OF WINDSWEPT PACIFIC and GOTTAHAVEABLE MUSIC
All Rights for RONDOR MUSIC (LONDON) LTD. in the U.S. and Canada Controlled and Administered by ALMO MUSIC CORP.
All Rights for SONGS OF WINDSWEPT PACIFIC Administered by BMG RIGHTS MANAGEMENT (US) LLC
All Rights for GOTTAHAVEABLE MUSIC Administered by BPJ ADMINISTRATION, P.O. Box 218061, Nashville, TN 37221
All Rights Reserved   Used by Permission

Chorus

What hurts the most...

Verse

It's hard to deal...

Pre-Chorus

Get - tin' up...

Chorus

What hurts the most...

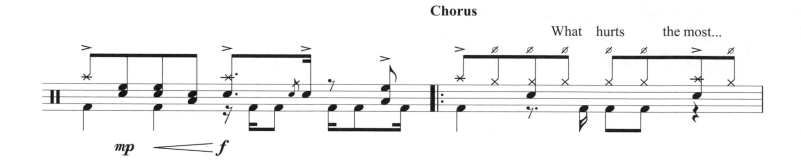

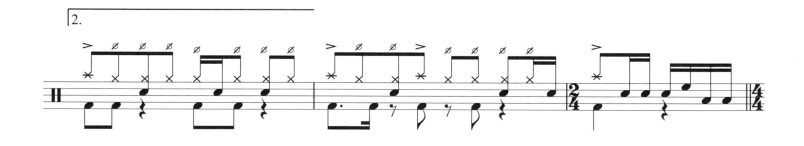

Guitar Solo

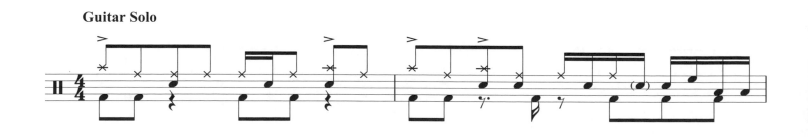

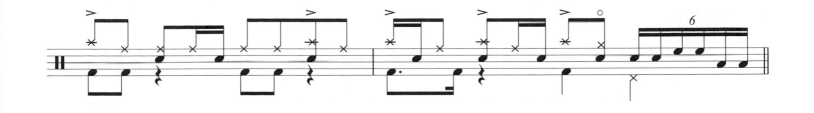

Chorus

What hurts   the most...

$mp < f$

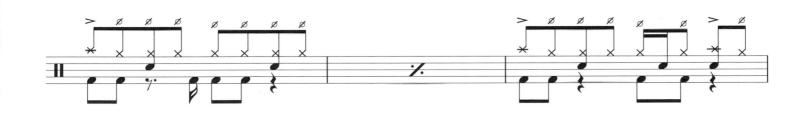

Outro

mp   *p*

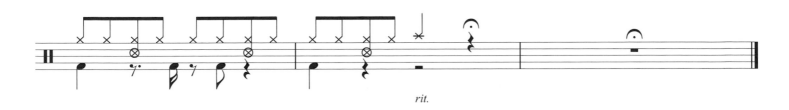

rit.

SMOOTH

Words by Rob Thomas
Music by Rob Thomas and Itaal Shur

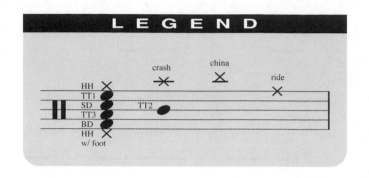

Copyright © 1999 EMI April Music Inc., EMI Blackwood Music Inc., U Rule Music and Itaal Shur Music
All Rights on behalf of EMI April Music Inc., EMI Blackwood Music Inc. and U Rule Music Administered by
Sony/ATV Music Publishing LLC, 424 Church Street, Suite 1200, Nashville, TN 37219
All Rights on behalf of Itaal Shur Music Administered by Downtown DMP Songs
International Copyright Secured   All Rights Reserved

Pre-Chorus

And if you said...

(4) *(8)*

Chorus

And it's just like the o - cean...

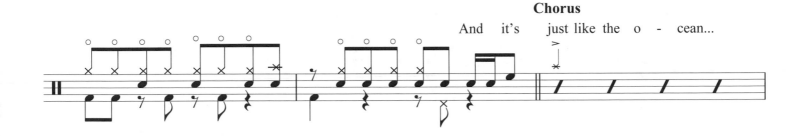

Interlude

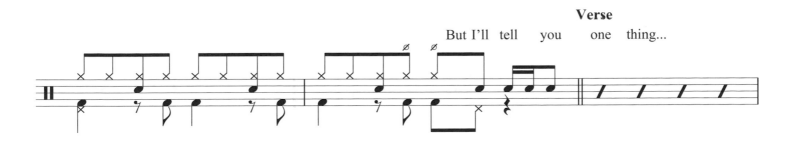

Verse

But I'll tell you one thing...

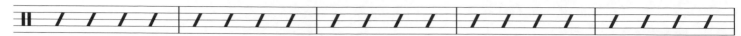

2

Pre-Chorus

And if you said...

(4)

And it's

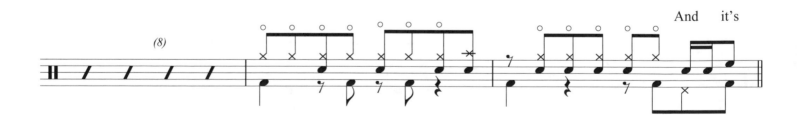

Chorus

just like the o - cean...

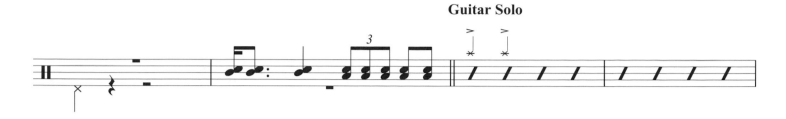

Guitar Solo

(4)

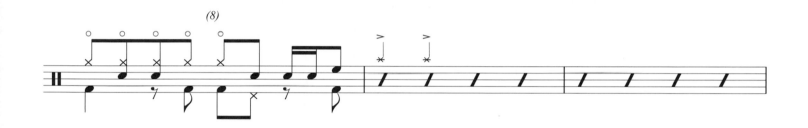

(8)

(12) *(16)*

Chorus

(4)

Outro-Guitar Solo

(4) *(8)*

(12)

(16) *(20)*

Fade out

(24)